18.95

EXTREME SPORTS

VERT SKATEBOARDING

BY CHRIS BOWMAN

EPIC

BELLWETHER MEDIA • MINNEAPOLIS, MN

EPIC BOOKS are no ordinary books. They burst with intense action, high-speed heroics, and shadows of the unknown. Are you ready for an Epic adventure?

This edition first published in 2016 by Bellwether Media, Inc.

No part of this publication may be reproduced in whole or in part without written permission of the publisher. For information regarding permission, write to Bellwether Media, Inc., Attention: Permissions Department, 5357 Penn Avenue South, Minneapolis, MN 55419.

Library of Congress Cataloging-in-Publication Data

Bowman, Chris, 1990-
 Vert Skateboarding / by Chris Bowman.
    pages cm. – (Epic: Extreme Sports)
 Includes bibliographical references and index.
 Summary: "Engaging images accompany information about vert skateboarding. The combination of high-interest subject matter and light text is intended for students in grades 2 through 7"– Provided by publisher.
 Audience: Grades 2 through 7.
 ISBN 978-1-62617-354-5 (hardcover : alk. paper)
 1. Skateboarding–Juvenile literature. 2. Extreme sports–Juvenile literature. 3. ESPN X-Games–Juvenile literature. I. Title.
 GV859.8.B68 2016
 796.22–dc23
                          2015033025

Printed in the United States of America, North Mankato, MN.

TABLE OF CONTENTS

WARNING

The tricks shown in this book are performed by professionals. Always wear a helmet and other safety gear when you are on a skateboard.

GOLD MEDAL RUN

Pierre-Luc Gagnon drops in for his second **run**. He is skating in the 2015 X Games Skateboard Vert event. He lands his first **trick** with ease. Then he pulls a Switch Heelflip 360.

Gagnon lands trick after trick. He finishes with a Nollie Heelflip 360. With this run, he wins X Games gold!

HARD TO BEAT
Pierre-Luc Gagnon's 2015 Vert win was his ninth X Games gold medal.

VERT SKATEBOARDING

"Vert" is short for **vertical**. Vert skateboarders ride on big halfpipes. These ramps have **steep** walls. Skaters ride the walls to gain speed. Then they do tricks above the lip.

VERT SKATEBOARDING TERMS

900—two and one-half spins in the air

carve—to turn sharply while keeping all four skateboard wheels on the riding surface

drop in—to begin skating down the ramp to start a run

halfpipe—a set of ramps that look like the bottom half of a pipe

lip—the top of the halfpipe

Nollie Heelflip 360—a trick in which the skater flips the skateboard while doing a full spin in the air

Switch Heelflip 360—a trick in which the skater flips the skateboard while doing a full spin in the air to land with the lead foot in back

VERT BEGINNINGS

Vert skateboarding began in Southern California. In the 1970s, skaters started riding in empty swimming pools. They carved around the pools' walls.

Vert skateboarding quickly grew more popular. But not all skaters lived near empty pools or skate parks. Some riders built halfpipes out of wood.

REINVENTING THE WHEEL

In 1970, Frank Nasworthy invented new skateboard wheels called Cadillacs. They made riding smoother and safer.

13

Halfpipes soon replaced swimming pools. Riders quickly came up with new tricks. Soon, the **innovative** new moves were used in **competitions**.

VERT GEAR

Vert skateboarding can be dangerous. All riders need to wear helmets, elbow pads, and knee pads. Wrist guards also keep skaters safe during falls.

NAILED IT

Vert ramps are not always perfectly smooth. Safety pads protect riders from nails and splinters that might stick out of the surface.

THE COMPETITION

Vert skateboarding competitions are held all over the world. Skateboarders land a series of tricks within a time limit. Each rider usually gets three runs.

AIR SPACE
Halfpipes used at competitions are often wide. This gives riders more space to do tricks.

EVENT SCORING

Judges may award skaters up to 100 points for a run. Each run is scored on its own. The run with the highest score wins the event.

Vert judges award points for **style**, difficulty, and **creativity**. Smooth runs and new tricks also earn more points. Daring riders continue to push the sport to new heights!

INNOVATOR OF THE SPORT

name: **Tony Hawk**
birthdate: **May 12, 1968**
hometown: **San Diego, California**
innovations: **Became the first rider to land a 900**

GLOSSARY

competitions—events that skateboarders try to win

creativity—having new ideas or doing something a different way

innovative—new and inventive

run—a turn at competing in an event

steep—almost straight up and down

style—the way something is done

trick—a specific move in a skateboarding event

vertical—straight up and down

TO LEARN MORE

AT THE LIBRARY

Adamson, Thomas K. *Big Air Skateboarding*. Minneapolis, Minn.: Bellwether Media, 2016.

Cain, Patrick G. *Skateboarding Vert*. Minneapolis, Minn.: Lerner Publications Company, 2013.

Craats, Rennay. *Skateboarding*. New York, N.Y.: AV2 by Weigl, 2014.

ON THE WEB

Learning more about vert skateboarding is as easy as 1, 2, 3.

1. Go to www.factsurfer.com.

2. Enter "vert skateboarding" into the search box.

3. Click the "Surf" button and you will see a list of related web sites.

With factsurfer.com, finding more information is just a click away.

INDEX